50 Salty Recipes for Home

By: Kelly Johnson

Table of Contents

- Classic Roast Chicken
- Spaghetti Bolognese
- Beef Tacos
- Chicken Parmesan
- Shrimp Scampi
- Bacon-Wrapped Asparagus
- Garlic Butter Shrimp
- Grilled Cheese Sandwich
- Beef Stir-Fry
- Margherita Pizza
- BBQ Pulled Pork
- Cajun Shrimp Pasta
- Beef and Broccoli
- Baked Ziti
- Lemon Garlic Roasted Chicken
- Buffalo Chicken Wings
- Chicken Alfredo
- Teriyaki Salmon
- Roasted Brussels Sprouts with Bacon
- Chili Con Carne
- Spinach and Feta Stuffed Chicken Breast
- Beef Fajitas
- Salt and Pepper Shrimp
- Italian Sausage and Peppers
- Chicken Fajitas
- Bacon-Wrapped Jalapeño Poppers
- Beef and Mushroom Stroganoff
- Sausage and Egg Breakfast Burritos
- Lemon Herb Grilled Salmon
- Teriyaki Chicken Skewers
- Classic Margarita
- Garlic Butter Steak Bites
- Chicken Satay with Peanut Sauce
- Ham and Cheese Stuffed Mushrooms
- Clam Linguine

- Mediterranean Chickpea Salad
- Pesto Shrimp Pasta
- Bacon-Wrapped Dates
- Lemon Pepper Grilled Chicken
- Spicy Korean Beef Bulgogi
- Salt and Vinegar Potato Wedges
- Chicken Piccata
- Pimento Cheese Stuffed Jalapeños
- Steak Tacos
- Greek Salad with Feta
- Bacon and Cheese Loaded Potato Skins
- Chicken and Rice Casserole
- Shrimp and Grits
- Salted Caramel Brownies
- Roasted Garlic and Parmesan Mashed Potatoes

Classic Roast Chicken

Ingredients:

- 1 whole chicken (about 3-4 pounds)
- Salt and pepper, to taste
- 2 tablespoons olive oil or melted butter
- 1 teaspoon dried thyme (optional)
- 1 teaspoon dried rosemary (optional)
- 1 teaspoon paprika (optional)
- 1 lemon, halved (optional)
- Fresh herbs (such as rosemary and thyme), for stuffing (optional)

Instructions:

Preheat your oven to 425°F (220°C).
Remove the giblets from the chicken cavity, if any, and pat the chicken dry with paper towels.
Season the chicken generously with salt and pepper, both inside and outside the cavity.
If desired, rub the outside of the chicken with olive oil or melted butter. This helps to achieve a golden and crispy skin.
Optional: Sprinkle dried thyme, rosemary, and paprika over the chicken for added flavor.
If using, stuff the chicken cavity with lemon halves and fresh herbs. This will infuse the chicken with aromatic flavors as it roasts.
Truss the chicken by tying the legs together with kitchen twine. This helps the chicken cook evenly.
Place the seasoned and trussed chicken in a roasting pan or on a wire rack set in a baking sheet.
Roast the chicken in the preheated oven for about 20 minutes per pound, plus an additional 15 minutes. Ensure the internal temperature reaches 165°F (74°C).
Once done, remove the chicken from the oven and let it rest for 10-15 minutes before carving.
Carve the roast chicken into desired pieces and serve with your favorite sides.

Enjoy your classic roast chicken!

Spaghetti Bolognese

Ingredients:

- 1 lb (450g) ground beef or a mixture of beef and pork
- 1 onion, finely chopped
- 2 cloves garlic, minced
- 1 carrot, finely chopped
- 1 celery stalk, finely chopped
- 1 can (14 oz/400g) crushed tomatoes
- 1/2 cup (120ml) red wine (optional)
- 1/2 cup (120ml) beef or vegetable broth
- 2 tablespoons tomato paste
- 1 teaspoon dried oregano
- 1 teaspoon dried basil
- 1/2 teaspoon dried thyme
- Salt and pepper to taste
- Olive oil
- 1 lb (450g) spaghetti

Instructions:

Heat a couple of tablespoons of olive oil in a large skillet or pot over medium heat.
Add chopped onions, garlic, carrots, and celery. Sauté until vegetables are softened.
Add the ground meat and cook until browned, breaking it apart with a spoon.
Pour in the wine (if using) and let it simmer for a couple of minutes until it's reduced.
Add crushed tomatoes, tomato paste, broth, oregano, basil, thyme, salt, and pepper. Stir well to combine.
Bring the mixture to a simmer, then reduce the heat to low, cover, and let it simmer for at least 30-45 minutes to allow the flavors to meld. You can simmer it longer if you have the time.
While the sauce is simmering, cook the spaghetti according to the package instructions. Drain and set aside.
Taste the Bolognese sauce and adjust the seasoning if necessary.

Serve the Bolognese sauce over the cooked spaghetti. You can also garnish with grated Parmesan cheese and fresh basil if desired.

Enjoy your delicious homemade Spaghetti Bolognese!

Beef Tacos

Ingredients:

For the seasoned beef:

- 1 lb (450g) ground beef
- 1 onion, finely chopped
- 2 cloves garlic, minced
- 1 tablespoon chili powder
- 1 teaspoon cumin
- 1/2 teaspoon paprika
- 1/2 teaspoon oregano
- Salt and pepper to taste

For serving:

- Taco shells (hard or soft)
- Shredded lettuce
- Diced tomatoes
- Shredded cheese (cheddar or Mexican blend)
- Sour cream
- Salsa or pico de gallo
- Chopped fresh cilantro
- Lime wedges

Instructions:

In a large skillet, cook the chopped onions until they become translucent.
Add minced garlic and cook for an additional 30 seconds until fragrant.
Add ground beef to the skillet and cook over medium heat, breaking it apart with a spoon, until browned.
Drain excess fat from the skillet if necessary.
Add chili powder, cumin, paprika, oregano, salt, and pepper to the beef. Stir well to evenly coat the meat with the seasonings. Cook for a few more minutes until the flavors meld.
While the beef is cooking, warm the taco shells according to the package instructions.
Assemble the tacos by spooning the seasoned beef into the taco shells.
Top the tacos with shredded lettuce, diced tomatoes, shredded cheese, sour cream, salsa or pico de gallo, and any other desired toppings.
Garnish with chopped fresh cilantro and serve with lime wedges on the side.

Enjoy your flavorful and customizable beef tacos! You can adjust the toppings based on personal preferences.

Chicken Parmesan

Ingredients:

For the chicken:

- 4 boneless, skinless chicken breasts
- Salt and pepper to taste
- 1 cup all-purpose flour
- 2 large eggs
- 2 cups breadcrumbs (Italian seasoned breadcrumbs work well)
- 1 cup grated Parmesan cheese
- Olive oil for frying

For assembling:

- 2 cups marinara sauce
- 1 cup shredded mozzarella cheese
- 1/4 cup grated Parmesan cheese
- Fresh basil or parsley for garnish (optional)

Instructions:

Preheat your oven to 375°F (190°C).
Season chicken breasts with salt and pepper.
Set up a breading station: Place flour in one shallow dish, whisk eggs in another dish, and combine breadcrumbs and grated Parmesan cheese in a third dish.
Dredge each chicken breast in flour, shaking off excess. Dip in beaten eggs, then coat with the breadcrumb-Parmesan mixture, pressing the crumbs onto the chicken to adhere.
Heat olive oil in a large skillet over medium-high heat. Fry the breaded chicken breasts until golden brown and cooked through, about 4-5 minutes per side.
Transfer the chicken to a paper towel-lined plate to drain excess oil.
In a baking dish, spread a thin layer of marinara sauce. Place the fried chicken breasts on top.
Spoon additional marinara sauce over each chicken breast.
Sprinkle shredded mozzarella cheese and grated Parmesan cheese over the top.

Bake in the preheated oven for 20-25 minutes or until the cheese is melted and bubbly.
Garnish with fresh basil or parsley if desired.

Serve the Chicken Parmesan over cooked pasta or with a side of crusty bread. Enjoy this comforting and flavorful dish!

Shrimp Scampi

Ingredients:

- 1 lb (450g) large shrimp, peeled and deveined
- Salt and pepper to taste
- 8 oz (225g) linguine or spaghetti
- 3 tablespoons unsalted butter
- 3 tablespoons olive oil
- 4 cloves garlic, minced
- 1/2 teaspoon red pepper flakes (optional)
- 1/2 cup (120ml) dry white wine
- 1/4 cup (60ml) chicken or vegetable broth
- Juice of 1 lemon
- Zest of 1 lemon
- 1/4 cup fresh parsley, chopped
- Grated Parmesan cheese for serving (optional)

Instructions:

Cook the pasta according to the package instructions. Drain and set aside.
Season the shrimp with salt and pepper.
In a large skillet, heat the butter and olive oil over medium heat.
Add minced garlic and red pepper flakes (if using) to the skillet. Sauté for about 1-2 minutes until the garlic becomes fragrant but not browned.
Add the seasoned shrimp to the skillet and cook for 2-3 minutes on each side until they turn pink and opaque. Be careful not to overcook the shrimp.
Pour in the white wine and chicken or vegetable broth. Simmer for 2-3 minutes to allow the alcohol to cook off.
Stir in lemon juice and zest, then add the cooked pasta to the skillet. Toss everything together to coat the pasta with the flavorful sauce.
Adjust the seasoning with salt and pepper if needed.
Garnish with chopped fresh parsley.
Serve the Shrimp Scampi immediately, optionally topped with grated Parmesan cheese.

Enjoy your quick and tasty Shrimp Scampi either on its own or over pasta!

Bacon-Wrapped Asparagus

Ingredients:

- 1 bunch of fresh asparagus spears
- 8-10 slices of bacon
- Olive oil
- Salt and pepper to taste
- Optional: Garlic powder, grated Parmesan cheese, or balsamic glaze for extra flavor

Instructions:

Preheat your oven to 400°F (200°C).
Wash and trim the tough ends off the asparagus spears.
Divide the asparagus into bundles, with 4-5 spears in each bundle.
Take a slice of bacon and wrap it around each bundle of asparagus, starting at one end and wrapping it diagonally to cover as much of the asparagus as possible.
Place the bacon-wrapped asparagus bundles on a baking sheet lined with parchment paper or aluminum foil.
Drizzle olive oil over the bacon-wrapped asparagus, and season with salt and pepper. Optionally, sprinkle with garlic powder or grated Parmesan cheese for added flavor.
Roast in the preheated oven for 20-25 minutes or until the bacon is crispy and the asparagus is tender. You can also broil for a few minutes at the end to get extra crispiness.
Remove from the oven and let it cool for a couple of minutes.
Optional: Drizzle with balsamic glaze before serving for a tangy touch.

Serve the bacon-wrapped asparagus as an appetizer or side dish. It's a crowd-pleaser with a perfect combination of flavors and textures. Enjoy!

Garlic Butter Shrimp

Ingredients:

- 1 lb (450g) large shrimp, peeled and deveined
- Salt and black pepper to taste
- 2 tablespoons olive oil
- 4 tablespoons unsalted butter
- 4 cloves garlic, minced
- 1/2 teaspoon red pepper flakes (optional)
- 1 tablespoon lemon juice
- 2 tablespoons chopped fresh parsley
- Lemon wedges for serving

Instructions:

Prepare Shrimp:
- Pat the shrimp dry with paper towels.
- Season the shrimp with salt and black pepper.

Cook Shrimp:
- Heat olive oil and 2 tablespoons of butter in a large skillet over medium-high heat.
- Add minced garlic and red pepper flakes (if using) to the skillet. Sauté for about 1 minute until the garlic becomes fragrant.

Sauté Shrimp:
- Add the seasoned shrimp to the skillet in a single layer.
- Cook for 2-3 minutes on one side until they start to turn pink, then flip and cook for an additional 2-3 minutes until fully cooked. Be careful not to overcook the shrimp.

Finish with Flavors:
- Add lemon juice to the skillet and stir to combine with the shrimp.
- Stir in the remaining 2 tablespoons of butter until melted and coats the shrimp evenly.

Garnish and Serve:
- Sprinkle chopped fresh parsley over the shrimp.
- Serve the Garlic Butter Shrimp immediately, either as an appetizer or over cooked pasta, rice, or with crusty bread.

Optional: Serve with Lemon Wedges:

- Serve the shrimp with lemon wedges on the side for an extra burst of citrus flavor.

Enjoy your flavorful and buttery Garlic Butter Shrimp!

Grilled Cheese Sandwich

Ingredients:

- 2 slices of bread (white, whole wheat, or your choice)
- 2 slices of your favorite cheese (cheddar, Swiss, American, etc.)
- Butter, softened

Optional add-ins:

- Cooked bacon
- Sliced tomatoes
- Sauteed onions
- Sliced ham
- Avocado slices

Instructions:

Preheat the Pan:
- Heat a skillet or griddle over medium heat.

Butter the Bread:
- Spread a thin layer of softened butter on one side of each slice of bread.

Assemble the Sandwich:
- Place one slice of bread, butter-side down, on a clean surface.
- Add the cheese slices on top of the bread.
- If you're adding any optional ingredients, now is the time to layer them on top of the cheese.
- Place the second slice of bread on top, butter-side up.

Grill the Sandwich:
- Carefully transfer the assembled sandwich to the preheated skillet or griddle.
- Cook for 2-3 minutes on each side, or until the bread is golden brown and the cheese is melted.
- You can press the sandwich down with a spatula to help the cheese melt evenly.

Serve:
- Once both sides are golden brown and the cheese is gooey, remove the sandwich from the heat.
- Let it cool for a minute, then slice it diagonally if desired.

Enjoy:
- Serve your grilled cheese sandwich while it's hot and gooey. It pairs well with a side of tomato soup or a simple salad.

Feel free to get creative with your grilled cheese sandwiches by trying different types of bread and cheese combinations or adding your favorite ingredients.

Beef Stir-Fry

Ingredients:

- 1 lb (450g) beef sirloin or flank steak, thinly sliced
- 2 tablespoons soy sauce
- 1 tablespoon oyster sauce
- 1 tablespoon hoisin sauce
- 1 tablespoon cornstarch
- 1 teaspoon sugar
- 2 tablespoons vegetable oil
- 3 cloves garlic, minced
- 1 tablespoon fresh ginger, grated
- 1 bell pepper, thinly sliced
- 1 cup broccoli florets
- 1 carrot, julienned
- 2 green onions, sliced (for garnish)
- Sesame seeds (optional, for garnish)
- Cooked rice or noodles for serving

Instructions:

Marinate the Beef:
- In a bowl, combine soy sauce, oyster sauce, hoisin sauce, cornstarch, and sugar. Add the thinly sliced beef to the marinade, ensuring the beef is well coated. Let it marinate for at least 15-20 minutes.

Prepare Vegetables:
- While the beef is marinating, prepare the vegetables by slicing the bell pepper, julienned the carrot, and cutting the broccoli into small florets.

Stir-Fry:
- Heat vegetable oil in a wok or large skillet over medium-high heat.
- Add minced garlic and grated ginger, sauté for about 30 seconds until fragrant.

Cook Beef:
- Add the marinated beef to the hot pan. Stir-fry for 2-3 minutes until the beef is browned and cooked through. Remove the beef from the pan and set it aside.

Cook Vegetables:

- In the same pan, add a bit more oil if needed. Stir-fry the sliced bell pepper, julienned carrot, and broccoli florets until they are crisp-tender.

Combine and Finish:
- Return the cooked beef to the pan with the vegetables. Toss everything together to combine and heat through.

Garnish and Serve:
- Garnish with sliced green onions and sesame seeds if desired.
- Serve the beef stir-fry over cooked rice or noodles.

Enjoy your homemade beef stir-fry, a tasty and quick meal with a perfect balance of flavors and textures!

Margherita Pizza

Ingredients:

- Pizza dough (store-bought or homemade)
- 1/2 cup pizza sauce (homemade or store-bought)
- 8 oz (about 225g) fresh mozzarella cheese, sliced
- 2-3 ripe tomatoes, thinly sliced
- Fresh basil leaves
- Extra-virgin olive oil
- Salt and black pepper to taste
- Cornmeal or flour for dusting

Instructions:

Preheat the Oven:
- Preheat your oven to the highest temperature it can go, usually around 475-500°F (245-260°C).

Prepare Pizza Dough:
- Roll out the pizza dough on a lightly floured surface to your desired thickness.

Assemble the Pizza:
- Transfer the rolled-out dough to a pizza stone or a baking sheet dusted with cornmeal or flour.
- Spread a thin layer of pizza sauce over the dough, leaving a small border around the edges.
- Arrange slices of fresh mozzarella and tomato on top of the sauce.

Bake the Pizza:
- Place the pizza in the preheated oven and bake for about 10-12 minutes or until the crust is golden and the cheese is melted and bubbly.

Add Fresh Basil:
- Remove the pizza from the oven and scatter fresh basil leaves over the hot pizza.

Drizzle with Olive Oil:
- Drizzle extra-virgin olive oil over the top of the pizza.

Season and Serve:
- Sprinkle with salt and black pepper to taste.
- Allow the pizza to cool for a few minutes before slicing and serving.

Enjoy your homemade Margherita pizza, a delicious and timeless classic! You can always customize it by adding a touch of garlic, a sprinkle of Parmesan, or a drizzle of balsamic glaze if desired.

BBQ Pulled Pork

Ingredients:

- 3-4 lbs (1.4-1.8 kg) pork shoulder or pork butt
- Salt and black pepper to taste
- 1 tablespoon smoked paprika
- 1 tablespoon brown sugar
- 1 teaspoon garlic powder
- 1 teaspoon onion powder
- 1 teaspoon cumin
- 1 teaspoon chili powder
- 1 cup (240 ml) chicken or vegetable broth
- 1 cup (240 ml) barbecue sauce (plus more for serving)
- Hamburger buns or sandwich rolls

Instructions:

Prepare the Pork:
- Trim excess fat from the pork shoulder or pork butt. Season it with salt and black pepper.

Make the Dry Rub:
- In a small bowl, combine smoked paprika, brown sugar, garlic powder, onion powder, cumin, and chili powder to create a dry rub.

Apply the Dry Rub:
- Rub the dry rub mixture all over the pork, ensuring it's well-coated.

Preheat the Slow Cooker:
- Place the seasoned pork in the slow cooker.

Add Broth:
- Pour the chicken or vegetable broth around the pork.

Slow Cook:
- Cover the slow cooker and cook on low for 8-10 hours or on high for 4-6 hours, or until the pork is very tender and easily shreds with a fork.

Shred the Pork:
- Remove the pork from the slow cooker and shred it using two forks.

Combine with BBQ Sauce:
- In a large bowl, combine the shredded pork with barbecue sauce. Adjust the amount of sauce to your liking.

Serve:

- Serve the BBQ pulled pork on hamburger buns or sandwich rolls.
- You can add extra barbecue sauce on top or serve with coleslaw for added freshness and crunch.

Enjoy your delicious and savory BBQ pulled pork sandwiches!

Cajun Shrimp Pasta

Ingredients:

- 8 oz (225g) linguine or fettuccine
- 1 lb (450g) large shrimp, peeled and deveined
- Cajun seasoning (store-bought or homemade)
- Salt and black pepper to taste
- 2 tablespoons olive oil
- 4 cloves garlic, minced
- 1 bell pepper, thinly sliced
- 1 cup cherry tomatoes, halved
- 1 cup heavy cream
- 1/2 cup chicken broth
- 1/2 cup grated Parmesan cheese
- Fresh parsley, chopped (for garnish)

Cajun Seasoning (optional):

- 1 tablespoon paprika
- 1 tablespoon onion powder
- 1 tablespoon garlic powder
- 1 teaspoon thyme
- 1 teaspoon oregano
- 1 teaspoon cayenne pepper (adjust to taste)
- Salt and black pepper to taste

Instructions:

Cook Pasta:
- Cook the pasta according to the package instructions. Drain and set aside.

Season Shrimp:
- Season the shrimp with Cajun seasoning, salt, and black pepper.

Sauté Shrimp:
- Heat olive oil in a large skillet over medium-high heat.
- Add the seasoned shrimp to the skillet and cook for 2-3 minutes per side or until they are opaque and cooked through. Remove shrimp from the skillet and set aside.

Sauté Vegetables:
- In the same skillet, add minced garlic, sliced bell pepper, and halved cherry tomatoes. Sauté for 2-3 minutes until the vegetables are slightly softened.

Prepare Cajun Seasoning (if not using store-bought):
- In a small bowl, mix together paprika, onion powder, garlic powder, thyme, oregano, cayenne pepper, salt, and black pepper.

Make the Sauce:
- Pour in the heavy cream and chicken broth, and stir in the Cajun seasoning (if not using store-bought). Allow the sauce to simmer for 2-3 minutes.

Add Cheese:
- Stir in grated Parmesan cheese until it's melted and the sauce has thickened.

Combine Pasta and Shrimp:
- Add the cooked pasta and sautéed shrimp to the skillet. Toss everything together until the pasta is coated in the creamy Cajun sauce.

Garnish and Serve:
- Garnish with chopped fresh parsley.
- Serve the Cajun Shrimp Pasta hot.

Enjoy your delicious and spicy Cajun Shrimp Pasta! Adjust the level of Cajun seasoning and cayenne pepper to suit your spice preference.

Beef and Broccoli

Ingredients:

- 1 lb (450g) flank steak or sirloin, thinly sliced
- 1/4 cup soy sauce
- 2 tablespoons oyster sauce
- 2 tablespoons hoisin sauce
- 1 tablespoon cornstarch
- 1 tablespoon brown sugar
- 1 cup beef broth
- 2 tablespoons vegetable oil (divided)
- 3 cloves garlic, minced
- 1 teaspoon fresh ginger, grated
- 4 cups broccoli florets
- Cooked white rice for serving
- Sesame seeds and sliced green onions for garnish (optional)

Instructions:

Marinate the Beef:
- In a bowl, mix soy sauce, oyster sauce, hoisin sauce, cornstarch, and brown sugar. Add thinly sliced beef to the marinade and let it marinate for at least 15-20 minutes.

Prepare Broccoli:
- Blanch the broccoli florets in boiling water for 2 minutes or until they are bright green. Drain and set aside.

Cook the Beef:
- Heat 1 tablespoon of vegetable oil in a wok or large skillet over medium-high heat.
- Add the marinated beef to the hot pan and stir-fry for 2-3 minutes until it's browned and cooked through. Remove the beef from the pan and set it aside.

Make the Sauce:
- In the same pan, add another tablespoon of oil if needed. Add minced garlic and grated ginger, sauté for about 30 seconds until fragrant.
- Pour in the beef broth and the remaining marinade. Stir and let it simmer for a couple of minutes until it thickens slightly.

Combine Beef and Broccoli:
- Add the cooked beef back to the pan, along with the blanched broccoli. Toss everything together until well-coated in the sauce and heated through.

Serve:
- Serve the Beef and Broccoli over cooked white rice.
- Garnish with sesame seeds and sliced green onions if desired.

Enjoy your homemade Beef and Broccoli, a delicious and satisfying dish with the perfect balance of flavors and textures!

Baked Ziti

Ingredients:

- 1 lb (450g) ziti pasta
- 1 lb (450g) ground beef or Italian sausage
- 1 onion, finely chopped
- 3 cloves garlic, minced
- 1 can (28 oz/800g) crushed tomatoes
- 1 can (15 oz/425g) tomato sauce
- 1 teaspoon dried oregano
- 1 teaspoon dried basil
- Salt and black pepper to taste
- 2 cups (480g) ricotta cheese
- 2 cups (200g) shredded mozzarella cheese
- 1/2 cup (50g) grated Parmesan cheese
- Fresh basil or parsley for garnish (optional)

Instructions:

Preheat the Oven:
- Preheat your oven to 375°F (190°C).

Cook the Ziti:
- Cook the ziti pasta according to the package instructions until it's just al dente. Drain and set aside.

Prepare the Sauce:
- In a large skillet, brown the ground beef or Italian sausage over medium heat. Add chopped onion and minced garlic, cooking until the onion is softened.
- Stir in crushed tomatoes, tomato sauce, dried oregano, dried basil, salt, and black pepper. Simmer for about 15-20 minutes to let the flavors meld.

Combine Pasta and Sauce:
- Mix the cooked ziti with the prepared sauce until well-coated.

Layering in Baking Dish:
- In a large baking dish, layer half of the ziti and sauce mixture. Dollop half of the ricotta cheese on top and sprinkle with half of the mozzarella and Parmesan cheese.

- Repeat the layers with the remaining ziti, sauce, ricotta, mozzarella, and Parmesan.

Bake:
- Bake in the preheated oven for 25-30 minutes or until the cheese is melted and bubbly, and the edges are golden brown.

Garnish and Serve:
- Remove from the oven and let it rest for a few minutes.
- Garnish with fresh basil or parsley if desired.
- Serve the Baked Ziti hot.

Enjoy your hearty and delicious Baked Ziti, a crowd-pleasing dish that's perfect for family dinners or gatherings!

Lemon Garlic Roasted Chicken

Ingredients:

- 1 whole chicken (about 4-5 lbs / 1.8-2.3 kg), giblets removed
- Salt and black pepper to taste
- 2 lemons, sliced
- 1 head of garlic, halved horizontally
- 2-3 sprigs of fresh rosemary or thyme
- 2 tablespoons olive oil
- 2 tablespoons melted butter
- 4 cloves garlic, minced
- 1 teaspoon dried oregano
- 1 teaspoon paprika

Instructions:

Preheat the Oven:
- Preheat your oven to 425°F (220°C).

Prepare the Chicken:
- Pat the chicken dry with paper towels. Season the cavity with salt and black pepper.
- Stuff the cavity with lemon slices, garlic halves, and fresh rosemary or thyme.

Season the Skin:
- In a small bowl, mix melted butter, olive oil, minced garlic, dried oregano, paprika, salt, and black pepper.

Rub the Chicken:
- Rub the chicken all over with the prepared butter and herb mixture. Ensure it's well coated, including under the skin.

Tie the Legs:
- If your chicken has a pop-up timer, leave it. Tie the chicken legs together with kitchen twine for even roasting.

Roasting:
- Place the chicken on a roasting pan or a baking dish with a rack.
- Roast in the preheated oven for about 1 hour and 15 minutes to 1 hour and 30 minutes, or until the internal temperature reaches 165°F (74°C) in the thickest part of the thigh without touching the bone.

Basting:
- Baste the chicken with the pan juices every 30 minutes to keep it moist.

Resting:
- Once done, tent the chicken with foil and let it rest for about 15 minutes before carving.

Carve and Serve:
- Carve the chicken and serve with the roasted lemon slices, garlic, and pan juices.

Enjoy your flavorful and succulent Lemon Garlic Roasted Chicken! It pairs well with roasted vegetables, potatoes, or a fresh salad.

Buffalo Chicken Wings

Ingredients:

For the Wings:

- 2 lbs (about 1 kg) chicken wings, split at joints, tips discarded
- Salt and black pepper to taste
- 1 cup all-purpose flour
- Vegetable oil for frying

For the Buffalo Sauce:

- 1/2 cup (115g) unsalted butter
- 1/2 cup hot sauce (like Frank's RedHot)
- 1 tablespoon white vinegar
- 1/4 teaspoon Worcestershire sauce
- 1/4 teaspoon cayenne pepper (optional, for extra heat)
- Garlic powder and onion powder to taste (optional)

Instructions:

Preheat the Oil:
- In a deep fryer or large, deep skillet, heat vegetable oil to 375°F (190°C).

Season and Coat the Wings:
- Season chicken wings with salt and black pepper. Dredge the wings in flour, shaking off excess.

Fry the Wings:
- Carefully place the wings in the hot oil, frying in batches for about 10-12 minutes or until golden brown and crispy. Ensure they are cooked through.

Drain and Rest:
- Remove the wings and place them on a paper towel-lined plate to drain excess oil.

Prepare the Buffalo Sauce:
- In a saucepan, melt the butter over medium heat. Add hot sauce, white vinegar, Worcestershire sauce, cayenne pepper, garlic powder, and onion powder. Stir until well combined and heated through.

Toss the Wings:
- In a large bowl, toss the fried wings in the prepared Buffalo sauce, ensuring they are evenly coated.

Serve:
- Serve the Buffalo Chicken Wings with celery sticks and your choice of dipping sauce (blue cheese dressing or ranch dressing are common choices).

Enjoy your delicious and spicy Buffalo Chicken Wings, a perfect appetizer for game days or gatherings! Adjust the heat level according to your preference.

Chicken Alfredo

Ingredients:

- 8 oz (225g) fettuccine pasta
- 1 lb (450g) boneless, skinless chicken breasts, cut into bite-sized pieces
- Salt and black pepper to taste
- 2 tablespoons olive oil
- 4 tablespoons unsalted butter
- 3 cloves garlic, minced
- 1 cup heavy cream
- 1 cup grated Parmesan cheese
- Salt and black pepper to taste
- Fresh parsley, chopped, for garnish (optional)

Instructions:

Cook the Pasta:
- Cook the fettuccine pasta according to the package instructions. Drain and set aside.

Season and Cook Chicken:
- Season the chicken pieces with salt and black pepper. In a large skillet, heat olive oil over medium-high heat. Add the chicken and cook until browned and cooked through, about 5-7 minutes. Remove the chicken from the skillet and set aside.

Make the Alfredo Sauce:
- In the same skillet, melt butter over medium heat. Add minced garlic and sauté for about 1 minute until fragrant.
- Pour in the heavy cream, stirring constantly, and bring it to a gentle simmer.

Add Parmesan Cheese:
- Reduce the heat to low. Gradually add the grated Parmesan cheese to the cream mixture, stirring continuously until the cheese is melted and the sauce is smooth.

Combine Chicken and Pasta:
- Return the cooked chicken to the skillet and toss until it's coated with the Alfredo sauce.

Season and Serve:

- Season the Chicken Alfredo with salt and black pepper to taste. Toss in the cooked fettuccine pasta and stir until the pasta is well coated in the sauce.

Garnish and Serve:
- Garnish with chopped fresh parsley if desired.
- Serve the Chicken Alfredo hot.

Enjoy your creamy and flavorful Chicken Alfredo! This dish pairs well with a side salad or some garlic bread.

Teriyaki Salmon

Ingredients:

- 4 salmon fillets
- Salt and black pepper to taste
- 1 tablespoon olive oil (for pan-searing)
- Sesame seeds and chopped green onions for garnish (optional)

For the Teriyaki Sauce:

- 1/4 cup soy sauce
- 2 tablespoons mirin (Japanese sweet rice wine)
- 2 tablespoons sake (or white wine)
- 2 tablespoons brown sugar
- 1 teaspoon grated fresh ginger
- 1 teaspoon minced garlic
- 1 teaspoon cornstarch mixed with 1 tablespoon water (optional, for thickening)

Instructions:

Prepare Teriyaki Sauce:
- In a small saucepan, combine soy sauce, mirin, sake, brown sugar, grated ginger, and minced garlic. Heat over medium heat until the sugar dissolves. If you want a thicker sauce, add the cornstarch-water mixture and stir until it thickens slightly. Remove from heat and set aside.

Preheat the Oven:
- Preheat your oven to 400°F (200°C).

Season Salmon:
- Pat the salmon fillets dry with paper towels. Season both sides with salt and black pepper.

Pan-Sear Salmon:
- In an oven-safe skillet, heat olive oil over medium-high heat. Place the salmon fillets in the skillet, skin side down, and sear for 2-3 minutes until the skin is crispy.

Brush with Teriyaki Sauce:
- Brush the top of each salmon fillet with the prepared teriyaki sauce.

Bake in the Oven:

- Transfer the skillet to the preheated oven and bake for about 8-10 minutes or until the salmon is cooked to your liking.

Broil (Optional):
- If you want to caramelize the top, you can broil the salmon for an additional 1-2 minutes until the sauce is slightly charred.

Garnish and Serve:
- Remove from the oven and brush more teriyaki sauce over the salmon.
- Garnish with sesame seeds and chopped green onions if desired.

Serve the Teriyaki Salmon over rice or with steamed vegetables for a delicious and balanced meal. Enjoy!

Roasted Brussels Sprouts with Bacon

Ingredients:

- 1 lb (450g) Brussels sprouts, trimmed and halved
- 4 slices bacon, chopped
- 2 tablespoons olive oil
- Salt and black pepper to taste
- 1-2 tablespoons balsamic vinegar (optional, for finishing)
- Grated Parmesan cheese for garnish (optional)

Instructions:

Preheat the Oven:
- Preheat your oven to 400°F (200°C).

Prepare Brussels Sprouts:
- Trim the ends of the Brussels sprouts and cut them in half. Remove any outer leaves that are discolored.

Cook Bacon:
- In a skillet over medium heat, cook the chopped bacon until it's crispy. Remove the bacon from the skillet and set it aside.

Toss Brussels Sprouts:
- In a large bowl, toss the halved Brussels sprouts with olive oil, salt, and black pepper until they are well coated.

Roast in the Oven:
- Spread the Brussels sprouts on a baking sheet in a single layer. Roast in the preheated oven for 20-25 minutes or until they are golden brown and crispy on the edges, tossing them halfway through.

Combine with Bacon:
- Remove the Brussels sprouts from the oven and toss them with the crispy bacon.

Optional Balsamic Finish:
- Drizzle balsamic vinegar over the roasted Brussels sprouts and bacon for added flavor.

Garnish and Serve:
- If desired, garnish with grated Parmesan cheese before serving.

Enjoy your Roasted Brussels Sprouts with Bacon as a tasty and satisfying side dish for any meal!

Chili Con Carne

Ingredients:

- 1.5 lbs (680g) ground beef
- 1 large onion, finely chopped
- 3 cloves garlic, minced
- 1 bell pepper, diced
- 2 cans (15 oz each) kidney beans, drained and rinsed
- 1 can (28 oz) crushed tomatoes
- 1 can (6 oz) tomato paste
- 2 cups beef broth
- 2 tablespoons chili powder
- 1 tablespoon ground cumin
- 1 teaspoon paprika
- 1 teaspoon oregano
- 1/2 teaspoon cayenne pepper (adjust to taste for spiciness)
- Salt and black pepper to taste
- 2 tablespoons vegetable oil
- Optional toppings: shredded cheese, sour cream, chopped green onions

Instructions:

Brown the Ground Beef:
- In a large pot or Dutch oven, heat vegetable oil over medium-high heat. Add ground beef and cook until browned, breaking it up with a spoon as it cooks.

Add Vegetables:
- Add chopped onions, minced garlic, and diced bell pepper to the pot. Cook for about 5 minutes until the vegetables are softened.

Season the Meat:
- Stir in chili powder, ground cumin, paprika, oregano, cayenne pepper, salt, and black pepper. Cook for an additional 2 minutes to allow the spices to bloom.

Add Tomato Products:
- Add crushed tomatoes, tomato paste, and beef broth to the pot. Stir well to combine.

Simmer:

- Bring the chili to a simmer, then reduce the heat to low. Cover and let it simmer for at least 30 minutes to allow the flavors to meld. You can simmer longer for even richer flavor.

Add Kidney Beans:
- Stir in the drained and rinsed kidney beans. Simmer for an additional 15-20 minutes.

Adjust Seasoning:
- Taste the chili and adjust the seasoning if needed. Add more salt, pepper, or spices according to your preference.

Serve:
- Ladle the chili into bowls. Serve hot with optional toppings like shredded cheese, sour cream, or chopped green onions.

Enjoy your hearty and flavorful Chili Con Carne! It's a great dish for gatherings and can be served with rice, cornbread, or tortilla chips.

Spinach and Feta Stuffed Chicken Breast

Ingredients:

- 4 boneless, skinless chicken breasts
- Salt and black pepper to taste
- 2 cups fresh spinach, chopped
- 1/2 cup crumbled feta cheese
- 2 tablespoons olive oil
- 2 cloves garlic, minced
- 1 teaspoon dried oregano
- 1 teaspoon dried thyme
- 1 teaspoon paprika
- Toothpicks or kitchen twine (to secure the chicken)

Instructions:

Preheat the Oven:
- Preheat your oven to 375°F (190°C).

Prepare Chicken Breasts:
- Lay each chicken breast flat on a cutting board. Use a sharp knife to make a horizontal slit along the side, creating a pocket in the chicken breast. Be careful not to cut all the way through.

Season and Stuff the Chicken:
- Season the inside and outside of each chicken breast with salt and black pepper.
- In a bowl, combine chopped spinach, crumbled feta, minced garlic, oregano, thyme, and paprika. Mix well.
- Stuff each chicken breast with the spinach and feta mixture, pressing the edges together to seal. Secure with toothpicks or kitchen twine if needed.

Sear the Chicken:
- Heat olive oil in an oven-safe skillet over medium-high heat. Once hot, add the stuffed chicken breasts and sear for 2-3 minutes on each side until golden brown.

Finish in the Oven:
- Transfer the skillet to the preheated oven. Bake for 20-25 minutes or until the chicken reaches an internal temperature of 165°F (74°C) and is no longer pink in the center.

Rest and Serve:
- Allow the stuffed chicken breasts to rest for a few minutes before slicing.

Serve:
- Slice the Spinach and Feta Stuffed Chicken Breast and serve. You can drizzle any pan juices over the top.

Enjoy your elegant and flavorful Spinach and Feta Stuffed Chicken Breast! This dish pairs well with a side salad, roasted vegetables, or quinoa.

Beef Fajitas

Ingredients:

For the Marinade:

- 1.5 lbs (680g) flank steak or skirt steak, sliced into thin strips
- 1/4 cup soy sauce
- 2 tablespoons olive oil
- 2 tablespoons lime juice
- 3 cloves garlic, minced
- 1 teaspoon ground cumin
- 1 teaspoon chili powder
- 1 teaspoon smoked paprika
- 1 teaspoon dried oregano
- Salt and black pepper to taste

For the Fajitas:

- 2 bell peppers, thinly sliced (use a mix of colors)
- 1 large onion, thinly sliced
- 2 tablespoons vegetable oil (for cooking)
- Flour or corn tortillas
- Optional toppings: salsa, guacamole, sour cream, shredded cheese, chopped cilantro, lime wedges

Instructions:

Marinate the Beef:
- In a bowl, combine soy sauce, olive oil, lime juice, minced garlic, ground cumin, chili powder, smoked paprika, dried oregano, salt, and black pepper. Add the sliced beef to the marinade, ensuring it's well-coated. Let it marinate for at least 30 minutes, or longer for more flavor.

Prepare Vegetables:
- Thinly slice the bell peppers and onions.

Cook the Fajitas:
- Heat vegetable oil in a large skillet or grill pan over medium-high heat.

- Add the marinated beef to the hot skillet and cook for 3-4 minutes until browned and cooked through. Remove the beef from the skillet and set it aside.

Sauté Vegetables:
- In the same skillet, add a bit more oil if needed. Add the sliced bell peppers and onions. Sauté for about 5-7 minutes until the vegetables are tender but still have a bit of crunch.

Combine Beef and Vegetables:
- Return the cooked beef to the skillet with the sautéed vegetables. Toss everything together until well combined and heated through.

Warm Tortillas:
- Warm the tortillas in a dry skillet or microwave according to package instructions.

Serve:
- Spoon the beef and vegetable mixture onto the warm tortillas.
- Add your favorite toppings, such as salsa, guacamole, sour cream, shredded cheese, chopped cilantro, and a squeeze of lime.

Enjoy your delicious and homemade beef fajitas! It's a customizable dish that's perfect for a fun and flavorful meal.

Salt and Pepper Shrimp

Ingredients:

- 1 lb (450g) large shrimp, peeled and deveined
- 1 cup cornstarch
- 1 teaspoon salt
- 1 teaspoon black pepper
- 1/2 teaspoon Chinese five-spice powder (optional)
- Vegetable oil for frying
- Green onions, chopped (for garnish)
- Red chili flakes (optional, for heat)
- Lemon wedges (for serving)

Instructions:

Prepare the Shrimp:
- Pat the shrimp dry with paper towels to remove excess moisture.

Coat with Cornstarch Mixture:
- In a bowl, mix together cornstarch, salt, black pepper, and Chinese five-spice powder (if using).
- Toss the shrimp in the cornstarch mixture, ensuring they are well-coated.

Heat Oil:
- In a wok or deep skillet, heat vegetable oil to around 350-375°F (175-190°C).

Fry the Shrimp:
- Carefully add the coated shrimp to the hot oil in batches. Fry for 2-3 minutes per batch until they turn golden brown and crispy. Make sure not to overcrowd the pan.

Drain and Season:
- Use a slotted spoon to remove the fried shrimp from the oil and place them on a paper towel-lined plate to drain excess oil.
- Immediately season the hot shrimp with a bit more salt and pepper.

Garnish and Serve:
- Garnish the Salt and Pepper Shrimp with chopped green onions and, if desired, red chili flakes for some heat.
- Serve the shrimp hot with lemon wedges on the side.

Enjoy your crispy and flavorful Salt and Pepper Shrimp as an appetizer or a tasty main dish! The combination of salt, pepper, and the crispy coating makes these shrimp a delightful treat.

Italian Sausage and Peppers

Ingredients:

- 1.5 lbs (680g) Italian sausages (sweet or hot), cut into links
- 2 tablespoons olive oil
- 1 large onion, thinly sliced
- 3 bell peppers (red, green, and yellow), thinly sliced
- 3 cloves garlic, minced
- 1 can (14 oz) crushed tomatoes
- 1 teaspoon dried oregano
- 1 teaspoon dried basil
- Salt and black pepper to taste
- 1/2 teaspoon red pepper flakes (optional, for heat)
- Fresh parsley, chopped (for garnish)
- Sub rolls or crusty Italian bread (for serving)

Instructions:

Cook the Sausages:
- In a large skillet or sauté pan, heat olive oil over medium-high heat. Add the Italian sausages and cook until browned on all sides. This will take about 8-10 minutes.

Sauté Peppers and Onions:
- Remove sausages from the skillet and set aside. In the same skillet, add sliced onions, bell peppers, and minced garlic. Sauté until the vegetables are softened, about 5-7 minutes.

Combine Sausages and Vegetables:
- Return the cooked sausages to the skillet with the sautéed peppers and onions.

Add Tomatoes and Seasoning:
- Pour in crushed tomatoes and add dried oregano, dried basil, salt, black pepper, and red pepper flakes (if using). Stir to combine.

Simmer:
- Reduce the heat to low, cover the skillet, and let it simmer for about 15-20 minutes, allowing the flavors to meld and the sausages to cook through.

Garnish and Serve:
- Garnish with chopped fresh parsley.

- Serve the Italian Sausage and Peppers hot, either on its own or in sub rolls or crusty Italian bread.

Enjoy your delicious and comforting Italian Sausage and Peppers! This dish is versatile and can be served as a main course, sandwich, or even over pasta or rice.

Chicken Fajitas

Ingredients:

For the Chicken Marinade:

- 1.5 lbs (680g) boneless, skinless chicken breasts, thinly sliced
- 3 tablespoons olive oil
- 2 tablespoons lime juice
- 1 teaspoon ground cumin
- 1 teaspoon chili powder
- 1 teaspoon smoked paprika
- 1 teaspoon garlic powder
- Salt and black pepper to taste

For the Fajitas:

- 1 large onion, thinly sliced
- 2 bell peppers, thinly sliced (use a mix of colors)
- 2 tablespoons vegetable oil
- Flour or corn tortillas
- Optional toppings: salsa, guacamole, sour cream, shredded cheese, chopped cilantro, lime wedges

Instructions:

Marinate the Chicken:
- In a bowl, combine olive oil, lime juice, ground cumin, chili powder, smoked paprika, garlic powder, salt, and black pepper. Add the sliced chicken, ensuring it's well-coated. Let it marinate for at least 15-20 minutes.

Cook the Chicken:
- Heat vegetable oil in a large skillet or wok over medium-high heat. Add the marinated chicken slices and cook for 5-7 minutes until fully cooked and slightly browned. Remove the chicken from the skillet and set it aside.

Sauté Vegetables:

- In the same skillet, add a bit more oil if needed. Add the sliced onions and bell peppers. Sauté for about 5-7 minutes until the vegetables are tender but still have a bit of crunch.

Combine Chicken and Vegetables:
- Return the cooked chicken to the skillet with the sautéed vegetables. Toss everything together until well combined and heated through.

Warm Tortillas:
- Warm the tortillas in a dry skillet or microwave according to package instructions.

Serve:
- Spoon the chicken and vegetable mixture onto the warm tortillas.
- Add your favorite toppings, such as salsa, guacamole, sour cream, shredded cheese, chopped cilantro, and a squeeze of lime.

Enjoy your delicious and homemade Chicken Fajitas! They are versatile, and you can customize them with your preferred toppings and extras.

Bacon-Wrapped Jalapeño Poppers

Ingredients:

- 12 large jalapeño peppers
- 8 oz (225g) cream cheese, softened
- 1 cup shredded cheddar or Monterey Jack cheese
- 1 teaspoon garlic powder
- 1 teaspoon onion powder
- 1/2 teaspoon smoked paprika
- Salt and black pepper to taste
- 12 slices of bacon, cut in half
- Toothpicks

Instructions:

Prepare Jalapeños:
- Preheat your oven to 375°F (190°C).
- Cut jalapeños in half lengthwise and remove the seeds and membranes. Wear gloves or wash your hands thoroughly after handling jalapeños to avoid irritation.

Prepare Filling:
- In a bowl, mix together softened cream cheese, shredded cheddar or Monterey Jack cheese, garlic powder, onion powder, smoked paprika, salt, and black pepper. Combine until smooth.

Fill Jalapeños:
- Spoon the cream cheese mixture into each jalapeño half, ensuring they are well-filled.

Wrap with Bacon:
- Wrap each jalapeño half with a half-slice of bacon. Secure with toothpicks to hold the bacon in place.

Bake:
- Place the bacon-wrapped jalapeño poppers on a baking sheet lined with parchment paper.
- Bake in the preheated oven for 20-25 minutes or until the bacon is crispy and the jalapeños are tender.

Broil (Optional):

- If the bacon needs more crisping, you can broil the poppers for an additional 1-2 minutes, watching closely to prevent burning.

Serve:
- Remove the toothpicks before serving.
- Serve the bacon-wrapped jalapeño poppers warm as an appetizer or party snack.

Enjoy your delicious and spicy bacon-wrapped jalapeño poppers! Adjust the level of heat by leaving more or fewer jalapeño seeds and membranes.

Beef and Mushroom Stroganoff

Ingredients:

- 1 lb (450g) beef sirloin or tenderloin, thinly sliced
- Salt and black pepper to taste
- 2 tablespoons olive oil
- 1 onion, finely chopped
- 2 cloves garlic, minced
- 8 oz (225g) cremini or white mushrooms, sliced
- 2 tablespoons all-purpose flour
- 1 cup beef broth
- 2 tablespoons Worcestershire sauce
- 1 tablespoon Dijon mustard
- 1/2 cup sour cream
- Fresh parsley, chopped, for garnish
- Cooked egg noodles or rice for serving

Instructions:

Season and Sear Beef:
- Season the sliced beef with salt and black pepper. In a large skillet, heat olive oil over medium-high heat. Add the sliced beef and sear until browned. Remove the beef from the skillet and set aside.

Sauté Onion and Mushrooms:
- In the same skillet, add chopped onion and minced garlic. Sauté until the onion is softened. Add sliced mushrooms and cook until they release their moisture and become golden brown.

Make the Sauce:
- Sprinkle flour over the mushroom mixture and stir well to combine. Cook for a minute to get rid of the raw flour taste.
- Gradually pour in beef broth, Worcestershire sauce, and Dijon mustard. Stir continuously to avoid lumps. Bring the mixture to a simmer and let it thicken.

Combine Beef and Sauce:
- Return the seared beef to the skillet. Stir in sour cream and let the mixture simmer for a few more minutes until the beef is cooked through and the sauce is creamy.

Adjust Seasoning:
- Taste and adjust the seasoning with more salt and pepper if needed.

Serve:
- Serve the Beef and Mushroom Stroganoff over cooked egg noodles or rice.
- Garnish with chopped fresh parsley.

Enjoy your comforting and flavorful Beef and Mushroom Stroganoff! It's a perfect dish for a cozy dinner.

Sausage and Egg Breakfast Burritos

Ingredients:

- 8 large flour tortillas
- 8 large eggs
- 1/2 lb (225g) breakfast sausage, crumbled
- 1 cup shredded cheddar cheese
- 1/2 cup diced bell peppers (any color)
- 1/4 cup diced onions
- Salt and black pepper to taste
- Salsa, sour cream, or hot sauce for serving (optional)
- Fresh cilantro or chopped green onions for garnish (optional)

Instructions:

Cook Sausage:
- In a skillet over medium heat, cook the crumbled breakfast sausage until browned and cooked through. Remove excess grease if necessary.

Sauté Vegetables:
- In the same skillet, add diced bell peppers and onions. Sauté until they are softened.

Scramble Eggs:
- Push the sausage and vegetables to one side of the skillet. Crack the eggs into the empty side and scramble them. Cook until they are just set.

Combine Ingredients:
- Mix the scrambled eggs with the cooked sausage and vegetables in the skillet. Season with salt and black pepper to taste.

Warm Tortillas:
- Heat the flour tortillas in a dry skillet or microwave for a few seconds to make them pliable.

Assemble Burritos:
- Place a portion of the egg and sausage mixture onto each tortilla. Sprinkle shredded cheddar cheese on top.

Roll Burritos:
- Fold in the sides of the tortilla and then roll it up to create a burrito.

Serve:

- Serve the Sausage and Egg Breakfast Burritos with salsa, sour cream, or hot sauce if desired.
- Garnish with fresh cilantro or chopped green onions.

Enjoy your delicious and hearty Sausage and Egg Breakfast Burritos! They are perfect for a quick and flavorful breakfast on the go.

Lemon Herb Grilled Salmon

Ingredients:

- 4 salmon fillets (about 6 oz/170g each), skin-on
- Salt and black pepper to taste
- 2 tablespoons olive oil
- Zest of 1 lemon
- Juice of 1 lemon
- 2 cloves garlic, minced
- 1 tablespoon fresh parsley, chopped
- 1 teaspoon fresh dill, chopped
- 1 teaspoon fresh thyme leaves
- Lemon wedges for serving

Instructions:

Preheat the Grill:
- Preheat your grill to medium-high heat.

Prepare the Marinade:
- In a bowl, whisk together olive oil, lemon zest, lemon juice, minced garlic, chopped parsley, chopped dill, and fresh thyme leaves.

Season the Salmon:
- Pat the salmon fillets dry with paper towels. Season both sides with salt and black pepper.

Marinate the Salmon:
- Place the salmon fillets in a shallow dish or a resealable plastic bag. Pour the marinade over the salmon, ensuring they are well-coated. Let it marinate for at least 15-30 minutes.

Grill the Salmon:
- Brush the grill grates with a bit of oil to prevent sticking.
- Place the marinated salmon fillets on the grill, skin-side down. Grill for about 4-5 minutes per side, or until the salmon is cooked through and easily flakes with a fork. You can also grill longer for a more well-done texture.

Serve:
- Transfer the grilled salmon to a serving platter.
- Serve the Lemon Herb Grilled Salmon with lemon wedges on the side.

Enjoy your light and flavorful Lemon Herb Grilled Salmon! It pairs well with a side of grilled vegetables, a fresh salad, or some quinoa.

Teriyaki Chicken Skewers

Ingredients:

- 1.5 lbs (680g) boneless, skinless chicken thighs, cut into bite-sized pieces
- Salt and black pepper to taste
- 1/2 cup soy sauce
- 1/4 cup mirin (Japanese sweet rice wine)
- 2 tablespoons sake (or white wine)
- 3 tablespoons honey or brown sugar
- 2 cloves garlic, minced
- 1 teaspoon grated fresh ginger
- 2 tablespoons vegetable oil (for brushing)
- Wooden skewers, soaked in water for 30 minutes

Instructions:

Prepare the Marinade:
- In a bowl, whisk together soy sauce, mirin, sake, honey (or brown sugar), minced garlic, and grated ginger.

Marinate the Chicken:
- Place the bite-sized chicken pieces in a shallow dish or a resealable plastic bag. Season with salt and black pepper. Pour half of the teriyaki marinade over the chicken and toss to coat. Reserve the other half for basting.

Marinate Time:
- Let the chicken marinate for at least 30 minutes to allow the flavors to infuse. You can marinate longer for more flavor, even overnight in the refrigerator.

Skewer the Chicken:
- Preheat your grill or oven (broiler).
- Thread the marinated chicken pieces onto the soaked wooden skewers.

Grill or Broil:
- Grill the skewers over medium-high heat for about 6-8 minutes, turning occasionally, or until the chicken is cooked through and has a nice char.
- If using the oven, place the skewers on a lined baking sheet and broil for 6-8 minutes, turning halfway through.

Baste with Marinade:

- While grilling or broiling, baste the chicken skewers with the reserved teriyaki marinade to add extra flavor.

Serve:
- Once cooked, remove the skewers from the grill or oven.
- Serve the Teriyaki Chicken Skewers hot, garnished with chopped green onions or sesame seeds if desired.

Enjoy your flavorful and succulent Teriyaki Chicken Skewers! They are great as an appetizer, party dish, or served over rice for a delicious meal.

Classic Margarita

Ingredients:

- 2 oz (60 ml) silver or blanco tequila
- 1 oz (30 ml) triple sec
- 3/4 oz (22.5 ml) fresh lime juice
- 1/2 oz (15 ml) simple syrup (optional, adjust to taste)
- Salt (for rimming the glass)
- Ice cubes

Instructions:

Prepare the Glass:
- If desired, rim the edge of a glass with salt. To do this, rub the rim with a lime wedge, then dip the rim into a plate with salt.

Mix the Margarita:
- In a shaker filled with ice, combine tequila, triple sec, fresh lime juice, and simple syrup (if using).
- Shake the mixture well for about 10-15 seconds to chill the ingredients.

Strain and Serve:
- Strain the Margarita mixture into the prepared glass over fresh ice.

Garnish (Optional):
- Garnish with a lime wheel or wedge on the rim of the glass.

Enjoy:
- Sip and enjoy your Classic Margarita!

Adjust the sweetness and tartness by modifying the amount of simple syrup and lime juice to suit your taste preferences. You can also experiment with different tequilas to find your preferred flavor profile.

Feel free to use a margarita glass or any other glassware you have available. Cheers!

Garlic Butter Steak Bites

Ingredients:

- 1.5 lbs (680g) sirloin or ribeye steak, cut into bite-sized cubes
- Salt and black pepper to taste
- 2 tablespoons olive oil
- 4 tablespoons unsalted butter
- 4 cloves garlic, minced
- 1 tablespoon fresh parsley, chopped (optional)
- Lemon wedges for serving (optional)

Instructions:

Prepare the Steak:
- Pat the steak cubes dry with paper towels to remove excess moisture. Season with salt and black pepper to taste.

Cook the Steak Bites:
- In a large skillet or pan, heat olive oil over medium-high heat. Add the steak cubes to the hot skillet and cook for 2-3 minutes on each side or until they reach your desired level of doneness.

Make the Garlic Butter Sauce:
- Reduce the heat to medium. Add unsalted butter to the skillet and let it melt. Stir in minced garlic and cook for about 1-2 minutes until the garlic is fragrant and slightly golden. Be careful not to burn the garlic.

Coat the Steak:
- Add the cooked steak bites back to the skillet. Toss them in the garlic butter sauce until they are well-coated.

Finish and Garnish:
- Sprinkle chopped fresh parsley over the steak bites for added flavor and freshness.

Serve:
- Serve the Garlic Butter Steak Bites hot, either as an appetizer or a main course.
- Optionally, squeeze a bit of fresh lemon juice over the steak bites before serving.

Enjoy your indulgent and flavorful Garlic Butter Steak Bites! They pair well with mashed potatoes, rice, or a side of vegetables.

Chicken Satay with Peanut Sauce

Ingredients:

For Chicken Satay:

- 1.5 lbs (680g) boneless, skinless chicken thighs or chicken breast, cut into thin strips
- 1/4 cup soy sauce
- 2 tablespoons fish sauce
- 2 tablespoons curry powder
- 2 tablespoons brown sugar
- 2 cloves garlic, minced
- 1 tablespoon vegetable oil
- Bamboo skewers, soaked in water for 30 minutes

For Peanut Sauce:

- 1/2 cup peanut butter
- 1/4 cup coconut milk
- 2 tablespoons soy sauce
- 1 tablespoon brown sugar
- 1 tablespoon lime juice
- 1 teaspoon curry powder
- 1 clove garlic, minced
- Water (to thin the sauce, as needed)

Instructions:

For Chicken Satay:

    Prepare Marinade:
- In a bowl, mix together soy sauce, fish sauce, curry powder, brown sugar, minced garlic, and vegetable oil.

    Marinate Chicken:
- Add the chicken strips to the marinade and coat them evenly. Let it marinate for at least 30 minutes, or longer for more flavor.

    Skewer Chicken:
- Thread the marinated chicken strips onto soaked bamboo skewers.

    Grill or Broil:

- Grill the skewers on an outdoor grill or broil in the oven for about 5-7 minutes on each side, or until the chicken is fully cooked and has a nice char.

For Peanut Sauce:

Prepare Peanut Sauce:
- In a saucepan over medium heat, combine peanut butter, coconut milk, soy sauce, brown sugar, lime juice, curry powder, and minced garlic.

Simmer and Thin:
- Heat the mixture, stirring constantly, until it becomes smooth and well combined. If the sauce is too thick, you can thin it with a little water to achieve your desired consistency.

Serve:
- Serve the grilled Chicken Satay with Peanut Sauce on the side for dipping.

Enjoy your flavorful Chicken Satay with Peanut Sauce! It makes a fantastic appetizer or main dish for any occasion.

Ham and Cheese Stuffed Mushrooms

Ingredients:

- 12 large white mushrooms, cleaned and stems removed
- 1/2 cup cooked ham, finely chopped
- 1/2 cup shredded mozzarella cheese
- 1/4 cup grated Parmesan cheese
- 2 tablespoons cream cheese, softened
- 2 cloves garlic, minced
- 1 tablespoon fresh parsley, chopped
- Salt and black pepper to taste
- Olive oil for brushing
- Fresh chives or additional parsley for garnish (optional)

Instructions:

Preheat the Oven:
- Preheat your oven to 375°F (190°C).

Prepare the Mushrooms:
- Clean the mushrooms and remove the stems. Place the mushroom caps on a baking sheet.

Make the Filling:
- In a bowl, combine chopped ham, mozzarella cheese, Parmesan cheese, softened cream cheese, minced garlic, chopped parsley, salt, and black pepper. Mix well to create a uniform filling.

Stuff the Mushrooms:
- Spoon the filling into the mushroom caps, pressing it down slightly.

Brush with Olive Oil:
- Brush the outside of the stuffed mushrooms with olive oil to help them brown during baking.

Bake:
- Bake in the preheated oven for about 15-20 minutes, or until the mushrooms are cooked through, and the filling is melted and golden.

Garnish and Serve:
- Remove from the oven and garnish with fresh chives or additional chopped parsley if desired.
- Serve the Ham and Cheese Stuffed Mushrooms warm.

These stuffed mushrooms make a great appetizer for parties, gatherings, or as a tasty snack. Enjoy!

Clam Linguine

Ingredients:

- 12 oz (340g) linguine pasta
- 2 tablespoons olive oil
- 4 cloves garlic, minced
- 1/2 teaspoon red pepper flakes (adjust to taste)
- 1 cup dry white wine
- 2 cans (10 oz each) whole baby clams, undrained
- 1/2 cup clam juice (reserved from the canned clams)
- Salt and black pepper to taste
- 1/4 cup fresh parsley, chopped
- Grated Parmesan cheese for serving (optional)

Instructions:

Cook Linguine:
- Cook the linguine pasta in a large pot of salted boiling water according to the package instructions until al dente. Drain and set aside.

Sauté Garlic and Red Pepper Flakes:
- In a large skillet, heat olive oil over medium heat. Add minced garlic and red pepper flakes. Sauté for about 1-2 minutes until the garlic becomes fragrant.

Add Wine and Clam Juice:
- Pour in the white wine and bring it to a simmer. Allow it to cook for a couple of minutes to reduce slightly.
- Add the clam juice from the canned clams and continue to simmer.

Add Clams:
- Add the whole baby clams with their juices to the skillet. Stir to combine and let them heat through for a few minutes.

Season and Toss:
- Season the sauce with salt and black pepper to taste. Toss the cooked linguine into the skillet, ensuring it's well coated with the clam sauce.

Finish and Garnish:
- Stir in chopped fresh parsley. Cook for an additional minute to let the flavors meld.

Serve:

- Serve the Clam Linguine hot, optionally topped with grated Parmesan cheese.

Enjoy your delicious and briny Clam Linguine! It's a simple and elegant dish that brings the flavors of the sea to your dinner table.

Mediterranean Chickpea Salad

Ingredients:

For the Salad:

- 2 cans (15 oz each) chickpeas, drained and rinsed
- 1 cucumber, diced
- 1 cup cherry tomatoes, halved
- 1 bell pepper (red, yellow, or orange), diced
- 1/2 red onion, finely chopped
- 1/2 cup Kalamata olives, pitted and sliced
- 1/2 cup feta cheese, crumbled
- 1/4 cup fresh parsley, chopped

For the Dressing:

- 1/4 cup extra-virgin olive oil
- 2 tablespoons red wine vinegar
- 1 teaspoon Dijon mustard
- 1 clove garlic, minced
- 1 teaspoon dried oregano
- Salt and black pepper to taste

Instructions:

Prepare Chickpeas:
- Rinse and drain the chickpeas thoroughly.

Chop Vegetables:
- In a large bowl, combine diced cucumber, cherry tomatoes, bell pepper, red onion, Kalamata olives, and fresh parsley.

Add Chickpeas:
- Add the drained chickpeas to the bowl with the vegetables.

Make the Dressing:
- In a small bowl, whisk together extra-virgin olive oil, red wine vinegar, Dijon mustard, minced garlic, dried oregano, salt, and black pepper.

Combine and Toss:

- Pour the dressing over the chickpea and vegetable mixture. Toss everything together until well combined and evenly coated with the dressing.

Add Feta:
- Gently fold in the crumbled feta cheese.

Chill (Optional):
- Allow the salad to chill in the refrigerator for about 30 minutes before serving to enhance the flavors.

Serve:
- Serve the Mediterranean Chickpea Salad as a side dish, light lunch, or a refreshing summer salad.

Enjoy your vibrant and flavorful Mediterranean Chickpea Salad! It's a perfect dish for picnics, potlucks, or a healthy meal at home.

Pesto Shrimp Pasta

Ingredients:

- 8 oz (about 225g) linguine or your preferred pasta
- 1 lb (about 450g) large shrimp, peeled and deveined
- Salt and black pepper to taste
- 2 tablespoons olive oil
- 4 cloves garlic, minced
- 1/2 cup cherry tomatoes, halved
- 1/3 cup basil pesto (store-bought or homemade)
- 1/4 cup grated Parmesan cheese
- Fresh basil leaves for garnish (optional)
- Red pepper flakes for a bit of heat (optional)

Instructions:

Cook Pasta:
- Cook the pasta according to the package instructions in a large pot of salted boiling water until al dente. Drain and set aside.

Season and Cook Shrimp:
- Season the shrimp with salt and black pepper. In a large skillet, heat olive oil over medium-high heat. Add minced garlic and cook for about 1 minute until fragrant.
- Add the seasoned shrimp to the skillet and cook for 2-3 minutes on each side or until they turn pink and opaque. Be careful not to overcook.

Add Tomatoes:
- Add halved cherry tomatoes to the skillet and cook for an additional 1-2 minutes until they start to soften.

Combine with Pasta:
- Reduce the heat to low. Stir in basil pesto, making sure the shrimp and tomatoes are evenly coated.
- Add the cooked pasta to the skillet and toss everything together until well combined.

Finish and Garnish:
- Sprinkle grated Parmesan cheese over the pasta and toss again to incorporate.

- If desired, garnish with fresh basil leaves and red pepper flakes for a bit of heat.

Serve:
- Serve the Pesto Shrimp Pasta immediately, with additional Parmesan on the side if desired.

Enjoy your delicious and flavorful Pesto Shrimp Pasta! It's a quick and satisfying dish that's perfect for a weeknight dinner.

Bacon-Wrapped Dates

Ingredients:

- Medjool dates, pitted (one for each bacon strip)
- Sliced bacon, cut in half (one slice for each date)
- Almonds or whole pecans (optional, one for each date)

Instructions:

Preheat the Oven:
- Preheat your oven to 375°F (190°C).

Prepare the Dates:
- If the dates still have pits, make a lengthwise slit in each date and remove the pit. If using almonds or pecans, stuff each date with a nut.

Wrap with Bacon:
- Take a half-slice of bacon and wrap it around each date, securing it with a toothpick if needed. If using nuts, make sure the nut is enclosed within the date.

Arrange on a Baking Sheet:
- Place the bacon-wrapped dates on a baking sheet lined with parchment paper, seam side down.

Bake:
- Bake in the preheated oven for about 15-20 minutes or until the bacon is crispy. You can also broil for the last couple of minutes to achieve extra crispiness.

Serve:
- Remove the toothpicks before serving.
- Serve the Bacon-Wrapped Dates warm as an appetizer.

These sweet and savory Bacon-Wrapped Dates are perfect for parties, gatherings, or as a delicious snack. The combination of flavors and textures makes them a delightful treat.

Lemon Pepper Grilled Chicken

Ingredients:

- 4 boneless, skinless chicken breasts
- Salt to taste
- 2 tablespoons olive oil
- Zest of 1 lemon
- Juice of 2 lemons
- 1 teaspoon black pepper (adjust to taste)
- 1 teaspoon garlic powder
- 1 teaspoon dried oregano or thyme (optional)
- Fresh parsley for garnish (optional)

Instructions:

Preheat the Grill:
- Preheat your grill to medium-high heat.

Prepare the Chicken:
- Pat the chicken breasts dry with paper towels. Season both sides with salt.

Prepare the Marinade:
- In a bowl, whisk together olive oil, lemon zest, lemon juice, black pepper, garlic powder, and dried oregano or thyme if using.

Marinate the Chicken:
- Place the chicken breasts in a shallow dish or a resealable plastic bag. Pour the marinade over the chicken, ensuring that each piece is well-coated. Let it marinate for at least 30 minutes to allow the flavors to infuse.

Grill the Chicken:
- Grease the grill grates to prevent sticking. Grill the chicken breasts for about 6-8 minutes per side or until they are fully cooked and have nice grill marks. The internal temperature should reach 165°F (74°C).

Rest and Garnish:
- Remove the chicken from the grill and let it rest for a few minutes before slicing.
- Garnish with fresh parsley if desired.

Serve:

- Serve the Lemon Pepper Grilled Chicken with your favorite side dishes, such as grilled vegetables, rice, or a fresh salad.

Enjoy your delicious and zesty Lemon Pepper Grilled Chicken! It's a perfect dish for a light and flavorful meal.

Spicy Korean Beef Bulgogi

Ingredients:

- 1 lb (450g) thinly sliced beef (ribeye or sirloin)
- 1/2 onion, thinly sliced
- 3 green onions, chopped
- 2 tablespoons sesame oil
- 2 tablespoons soy sauce
- 2 tablespoons gochugaru (Korean red pepper flakes) - adjust to your spice preference
- 2 tablespoons sugar
- 1 tablespoon mirin or rice wine
- 1 tablespoon minced garlic
- 1 teaspoon grated ginger
- 1 tablespoon toasted sesame seeds (for garnish)
- Cooked rice (for serving)

Instructions:

Prepare the Marinade:
- In a bowl, mix together sesame oil, soy sauce, gochugaru, sugar, mirin, minced garlic, and grated ginger to create the marinade.

Marinate the Beef:
- Place the thinly sliced beef, onion slices, and chopped green onions in a large bowl. Pour the marinade over the beef and mix well, ensuring all slices are coated. Let it marinate for at least 30 minutes to allow the flavors to meld.

Cook the Bulgogi:
- Heat a large skillet or wok over medium-high heat. Add the marinated beef and onions to the skillet. Stir-fry for 5-7 minutes or until the beef is fully cooked and the onions are tender.

Garnish and Serve:
- Garnish the Bulgogi with toasted sesame seeds and additional chopped green onions.
- Serve the Spicy Korean Beef Bulgogi over cooked rice.

Enjoy your Spicy Korean Beef Bulgogi! It's a delightful and satisfying dish with a perfect balance of sweet, savory, and spicy flavors.

Salt and Vinegar Potato Wedges

Ingredients:

- 4 large russet potatoes, washed and cut into wedges
- 1 cup white vinegar
- 2 tablespoons olive oil
- 1 teaspoon salt (plus extra for sprinkling)
- 1/2 teaspoon black pepper
- 1 tablespoon fresh parsley, chopped (optional, for garnish)

Instructions:

Preheat the Oven:
- Preheat your oven to 425°F (220°C).

Boil Potatoes in Vinegar:
- In a large pot, bring the white vinegar to a boil. Add the potato wedges and boil for about 5-7 minutes. This step helps infuse the potatoes with the vinegar flavor.

Drain and Dry:
- Drain the potatoes and pat them dry with paper towels. Allow them to air-dry for a few minutes.

Coat with Olive Oil:
- Place the dried potato wedges on a baking sheet. Drizzle them with olive oil and toss to coat evenly.

Season:
- Sprinkle the potato wedges with salt and black pepper, ensuring they are well-seasoned.

Bake:
- Bake in the preheated oven for about 25-30 minutes or until the wedges are golden brown and crispy. Flip the wedges halfway through the baking time to ensure even cooking.

Garnish and Serve:
- Once out of the oven, sprinkle the Salt and Vinegar Potato Wedges with a little more salt for extra flavor.
- Optionally, garnish with chopped fresh parsley.

Serve:
- Serve the wedges hot as a side dish or snack.

Enjoy your tangy and crispy Salt and Vinegar Potato Wedges! They make a tasty and unique alternative to regular potato wedges.

Chicken Piccata

Ingredients:

- 4 boneless, skinless chicken breasts
- Salt and black pepper to taste
- 1/2 cup all-purpose flour, for dredging
- 4 tablespoons unsalted butter, divided
- 2 tablespoons olive oil
- 1/3 cup fresh lemon juice (about 2 lemons)
- 1/2 cup chicken broth
- 1/4 cup capers, drained
- 1/4 cup fresh parsley, chopped
- Lemon slices for garnish (optional)

Instructions:

Prepare the Chicken:
- Season the chicken breasts with salt and black pepper on both sides.
- Dredge the chicken in flour, shaking off excess.

Cook the Chicken:
- In a large skillet, heat 2 tablespoons of butter and olive oil over medium-high heat. Add the chicken breasts and cook for about 3-4 minutes per side or until they are golden brown and cooked through. Remove the chicken from the skillet and set aside.

Make the Sauce:
- In the same skillet, add the lemon juice, chicken broth, and capers. Scrape any browned bits from the bottom of the skillet. Bring the sauce to a simmer.

Finish Cooking:
- Return the cooked chicken to the skillet and simmer for an additional 2-3 minutes to heat through and allow the flavors to meld.

Add Butter and Garnish:
- Stir in the remaining 2 tablespoons of butter until the sauce is smooth and glossy. Stir in chopped parsley.
- Optionally, garnish with lemon slices.

Serve:
- Serve the Chicken Piccata over pasta, rice, or with your favorite side dish.

Enjoy your delicious and zesty Chicken Piccata! It's a delightful dish with a perfect balance of flavors.

Pimento Cheese Stuffed Jalapeños

Ingredients:

- 12-15 fresh jalapeños
- 1 cup pimento cheese (store-bought or homemade)
- 1/2 cup shredded cheddar cheese (optional, for topping)
- Bacon strips (optional, for wrapping)
- Toothpicks (if using bacon)

Instructions:

Preheat the Oven:
- Preheat your oven to 375°F (190°C).

Prepare Jalapeños:
- Cut the jalapeños in half lengthwise and remove the seeds and membranes. Use caution when handling jalapeños, and consider wearing gloves to protect your hands.

Fill with Pimento Cheese:
- Fill each jalapeño half with pimento cheese, smoothing the top with a spoon.

Optional: Wrap with Bacon:
- If desired, wrap each stuffed jalapeño with a strip of bacon and secure it with a toothpick.

Arrange on a Baking Sheet:
- Place the stuffed jalapeños on a baking sheet lined with parchment paper.

Bake:
- Bake in the preheated oven for about 15-20 minutes or until the jalapeños are tender and the cheese is melted and bubbly. If you wrapped them in bacon, the bacon should be crispy.

Optional: Top with Shredded Cheddar:
- If you like, sprinkle a bit of shredded cheddar cheese on top of each stuffed jalapeño during the last 5 minutes of baking.

Serve:
- Remove from the oven and let them cool slightly before serving.
- Serve the Pimento Cheese Stuffed Jalapeños as a spicy and cheesy appetizer.

These stuffed jalapeños are perfect for parties, game days, or any occasion where you want to add a kick of flavor to your appetizer spread. Enjoy!

Steak Tacos

Ingredients:

- 1.5 lbs (680g) flank steak or skirt steak
- 1 tablespoon olive oil
- 2 cloves garlic, minced
- 1 teaspoon ground cumin
- 1 teaspoon chili powder
- 1 teaspoon paprika
- 1 teaspoon onion powder
- Salt and black pepper to taste
- Corn or flour tortillas
- Toppings: Salsa, diced onions, chopped cilantro, lime wedges, shredded cheese, sour cream, avocado slices, etc.

Instructions:

Prepare the Steak:
- In a bowl, mix together olive oil, minced garlic, ground cumin, chili powder, paprika, onion powder, salt, and black pepper to create a marinade.

Marinate the Steak:
- Place the flank steak in a dish and rub the marinade over both sides of the steak. Let it marinate for at least 30 minutes, or refrigerate for a few hours or overnight for more flavor.

Grill or Cook the Steak:
- Preheat your grill or a skillet over medium-high heat. Grill the steak for about 4-6 minutes per side for medium-rare or to your desired doneness. Cooking time may vary based on thickness.

Rest and Slice:
- Remove the steak from the grill and let it rest for a few minutes. Slice the steak thinly against the grain.

Warm the Tortillas:
- Warm the tortillas on the grill or in a dry skillet for about 20 seconds on each side.

Assemble Tacos:
- Place slices of grilled steak in the center of each tortilla.

- Add your favorite toppings such as salsa, diced onions, chopped cilantro, cheese, sour cream, and avocado slices.

Serve:
- Serve the Steak Tacos with lime wedges on the side.

Enjoy your flavorful and customizable Steak Tacos! They are perfect for a quick and delicious meal.

Greek Salad with Feta

Ingredients:

- 1 cucumber, diced
- 2 large tomatoes, diced
- 1 red onion, thinly sliced
- 1 green bell pepper, diced
- 1 cup Kalamata olives, pitted
- 1 cup crumbled feta cheese
- 1/4 cup fresh parsley, chopped
- 1/4 cup extra-virgin olive oil
- Juice of 1 lemon
- 1 teaspoon dried oregano
- Salt and black pepper to taste

Instructions:

Prepare Vegetables:
- In a large salad bowl, combine diced cucumber, diced tomatoes, thinly sliced red onion, diced green bell pepper, Kalamata olives, and crumbled feta cheese.

Make the Dressing:
- In a small bowl, whisk together extra-virgin olive oil, lemon juice, dried oregano, salt, and black pepper to create the dressing.

Toss the Salad:
- Pour the dressing over the salad ingredients in the large bowl. Gently toss everything together until well combined.

Garnish:
- Sprinkle chopped fresh parsley over the salad for added flavor and freshness.

Chill (Optional):
- If time allows, refrigerate the Greek Salad for about 30 minutes to let the flavors meld.

Serve:
- Serve the Greek Salad with Feta as a refreshing side dish or a light and healthy meal.

Enjoy your crisp and vibrant Greek Salad with the richness of feta cheese! It's perfect for a quick lunch, dinner, or as a side at a summer gathering.

Bacon and Cheese Loaded Potato Skins

Ingredients:

- 4 large russet potatoes, scrubbed and dried
- 6 slices bacon, cooked and crumbled
- 1 cup shredded cheddar cheese (or your favorite cheese)
- 1/4 cup sour cream
- 2 green onions, sliced
- Salt and black pepper to taste
- Olive oil or melted butter for brushing

Instructions:

Preheat the Oven:
- Preheat your oven to 400°F (200°C).

Bake the Potatoes:
- Pierce each potato several times with a fork. Place the potatoes directly on the oven rack and bake for about 45-60 minutes or until the potatoes are tender when pierced with a fork.

Prepare Potato Skins:
- Allow the baked potatoes to cool slightly. Cut each potato in half lengthwise. Scoop out the flesh, leaving about 1/4 inch of potato attached to the skin.

Brush with Oil or Butter:
- Brush the inside and outside of the potato skins with olive oil or melted butter. Sprinkle with salt and black pepper.

Bake Again:
- Place the potato skins on a baking sheet and bake in the preheated oven for about 10-15 minutes or until they become golden and crispy.

Add Bacon and Cheese:
- Remove the potato skins from the oven. Fill each skin with shredded cheddar cheese and crumbled bacon.

Broil:
- Set the oven to broil and place the loaded potato skins back in the oven for 2-3 minutes or until the cheese is melted and bubbly.

Top and Serve:
- Remove from the oven and top with sour cream and sliced green onions.

Serve:
- Serve the Bacon and Cheese Loaded Potato Skins hot as a tasty appetizer or snack.

Enjoy your delicious and cheesy loaded potato skins! They are sure to be a hit at any gathering.

Chicken and Rice Casserole

Ingredients:

- 1.5 lbs (680g) boneless, skinless chicken breasts, cooked and shredded
- 2 cups white rice, cooked
- 1 cup frozen peas and carrots mix (or mixed vegetables of your choice)
- 1/2 cup diced onion
- 1/2 cup diced celery
- 1/2 cup diced bell pepper (any color)
- 2 cloves garlic, minced
- 2 tablespoons butter
- 2 tablespoons all-purpose flour
- 2 cups chicken broth
- 1 cup milk
- 1 teaspoon dried thyme
- 1 teaspoon dried rosemary
- Salt and black pepper to taste
- 1 cup shredded cheddar cheese (optional, for topping)
- Fresh parsley for garnish (optional)

Instructions:

Preheat the Oven:
- Preheat your oven to 350°F (175°C).

Prepare Ingredients:
- Cook and shred the chicken. Cook the rice according to package instructions. If using frozen peas and carrots, thaw them.

Sauté Vegetables:
- In a large skillet, melt butter over medium heat. Add diced onion, celery, bell pepper, and minced garlic. Sauté until the vegetables are softened.

Make the Sauce:
- Sprinkle flour over the sautéed vegetables and stir to coat. Cook for 1-2 minutes.
- Gradually whisk in chicken broth and milk to create a smooth sauce. Continue cooking, stirring constantly, until the mixture thickens.

Season:
- Stir in dried thyme, dried rosemary, salt, and black pepper.

Combine Ingredients:
- In a large mixing bowl, combine the shredded chicken, cooked rice, thawed peas and carrots, and the creamy sauce. Mix until well combined.

Transfer to Casserole Dish:
- Transfer the mixture to a greased 9x13-inch baking dish or a casserole dish of similar size.

Bake:
- Bake in the preheated oven for about 25-30 minutes or until the casserole is heated through and the top is golden.

Optional: Add Cheese Topping:
- If desired, sprinkle shredded cheddar cheese over the top during the last 10 minutes of baking, and let it melt and become bubbly.

Garnish and Serve:
- Remove from the oven, garnish with fresh parsley if desired, and serve the Chicken and Rice Casserole hot.

Enjoy your comforting and flavorful Chicken and Rice Casserole! It's a great one-dish meal that the whole family will love.

Shrimp and Grits

Ingredients:

For the Grits:

- 1 cup stone-ground grits
- 4 cups water
- 1 cup milk
- Salt to taste
- 2 tablespoons butter
- 1 cup shredded cheddar cheese (optional)

For the Shrimp:

- 1 lb (450g) large shrimp, peeled and deveined
- 2 tablespoons Cajun seasoning (store-bought or homemade)
- Salt and black pepper to taste
- 4 slices bacon, chopped
- 1 small onion, finely chopped
- 1 bell pepper, finely chopped
- 2 cloves garlic, minced
- 1 cup chicken broth
- 2 tablespoons fresh lemon juice
- Chopped green onions for garnish
- Fresh parsley for garnish

Instructions:

For the Grits:

    Cook Grits:
- In a medium saucepan, bring water, milk, and salt to a boil. Gradually whisk in the grits, reduce heat to low, and simmer. Stir frequently to prevent sticking. Cook until the grits are thick and creamy, about 20-25 minutes.

    Add Butter and Cheese:
- Once the grits are cooked, stir in butter and shredded cheddar cheese if using. Adjust salt to taste.

    Keep Warm:

- Keep the grits warm while preparing the shrimp.

For the Shrimp:

Season Shrimp:
- In a bowl, toss the peeled and deveined shrimp with Cajun seasoning, salt, and black pepper.

Cook Bacon:
- In a large skillet, cook the chopped bacon over medium heat until it becomes crispy. Remove bacon and set aside, leaving the drippings in the pan.

Sauté Vegetables:
- In the same skillet with bacon drippings, sauté finely chopped onion and bell pepper until they become tender. Add minced garlic and cook for an additional 1-2 minutes.

Cook Shrimp:
- Add the seasoned shrimp to the skillet and cook for 2-3 minutes on each side or until they are pink and cooked through.

Deglaze with Broth:
- Pour in chicken broth and fresh lemon juice, scraping the bottom of the skillet to incorporate the flavorful bits. Simmer for a couple of minutes to allow the sauce to thicken slightly.

Assemble:
- Spoon a generous portion of cheesy grits onto plates. Top with the cooked shrimp and the vegetable and broth mixture.

Garnish:
- Garnish with chopped green onions, crispy bacon, and fresh parsley.

Serve the Shrimp and Grits hot, and enjoy this delightful Southern comfort dish!

Salted Caramel Brownies

Ingredients:

For the Brownies:

- 1 cup (2 sticks) unsalted butter
- 2 cups granulated sugar
- 4 large eggs
- 1 teaspoon vanilla extract
- 1 cup all-purpose flour
- 1/2 cup unsweetened cocoa powder
- 1/4 teaspoon salt

For the Salted Caramel:

- 1 cup granulated sugar
- 6 tablespoons unsalted butter, cubed
- 1/2 cup heavy cream
- 1 teaspoon sea salt (adjust to taste)

Instructions:

For the Brownies:

   Preheat the Oven:
   - Preheat your oven to 350°F (175°C). Grease and line a 9x13-inch baking pan with parchment paper, leaving some overhang on the sides for easy removal.

   Melt Butter:
   - In a medium-sized saucepan, melt the butter over medium heat. Remove from heat.

   Add Sugar and Eggs:
   - Stir in sugar until well combined. Add eggs one at a time, mixing well after each addition. Stir in vanilla extract.

   Combine Dry Ingredients:
   - In a separate bowl, sift together flour, cocoa powder, and salt.

Mix Batter:
- Gradually add the dry ingredients to the wet ingredients, stirring until just combined. Be careful not to overmix.

Bake:
- Pour the brownie batter into the prepared baking pan. Smooth the top with a spatula. Bake in the preheated oven for 25-30 minutes or until a toothpick inserted into the center comes out with moist crumbs (not wet batter).

Cool:
- Allow the brownies to cool completely in the pan on a wire rack.

For the Salted Caramel:

Prepare Caramel Sauce:
- In a heavy saucepan, heat granulated sugar over medium heat. Stir continuously until the sugar melts and turns into a golden amber color.

Add Butter and Cream:
- Carefully add cubed butter to the melted sugar, stirring until well combined. Slowly pour in the heavy cream while stirring constantly. Be cautious, as the mixture will bubble up.

Add Salt:
- Stir in sea salt to taste. Allow the caramel sauce to simmer for a minute, then remove from heat.

Cool:
- Let the salted caramel cool slightly.

Assemble:

Pour Caramel Over Brownies:
- Pour the slightly cooled salted caramel over the cooled brownies in the baking pan.

Chill:
- Place the brownies in the refrigerator to allow the caramel to set for a few hours or overnight.

Cut and Serve:
- Once the caramel is set, use the parchment paper overhang to lift the brownies out of the pan. Cut into squares and serve.

Enjoy your decadent Salted Caramel Brownies! They are a delightful treat for any sweet and salty cravings.

Roasted Garlic and Parmesan Mashed Potatoes

Ingredients:

- 4 large russet potatoes, peeled and cut into chunks
- 1 head of garlic
- 2 tablespoons olive oil
- 1/2 cup grated Parmesan cheese
- 1/2 cup unsalted butter
- 1 cup warm milk
- Salt and black pepper to taste
- Chopped fresh parsley for garnish (optional)

Instructions:

Roast Garlic:
- Preheat your oven to 400°F (200°C).
- Cut the top off the head of garlic to expose the cloves. Place it on a piece of foil, drizzle with olive oil, and wrap it up. Roast in the oven for about 30-40 minutes or until the garlic cloves are soft and golden. Let it cool.

Cook Potatoes:
- In a large pot, bring salted water to a boil. Add the peeled and chopped potatoes and cook until fork-tender, about 15-20 minutes.

Mash Potatoes:
- Drain the potatoes and return them to the pot. Mash them using a potato masher or a fork.

Prepare Roasted Garlic:
- Squeeze the roasted garlic cloves out of their skins and add them to the mashed potatoes.

Add Butter and Parmesan:
- Add butter and grated Parmesan cheese to the mashed potatoes.

Mash and Mix:
- Mash and mix the potatoes, roasted garlic, butter, and Parmesan until well combined.

Add Warm Milk:
- Gradually add warm milk to the mashed potatoes while continuing to mix until you reach your desired creamy consistency.

Season:

- Season with salt and black pepper to taste. Adjust the ingredients if necessary.

Garnish and Serve:
- Garnish with chopped fresh parsley if desired.
- Serve the Roasted Garlic and Parmesan Mashed Potatoes hot.

These mashed potatoes are rich, creamy, and have a wonderful roasted garlic flavor with the added kick of Parmesan. They make a fantastic side dish for a variety of meals. Enjoy!